Printed in the United States of America.

First Printing, May 2021

ISBN 978-0-9904383-5-9

surveyingmanual@gmail.com

Texas State Specific Land Surveying:
Exam Study Manual

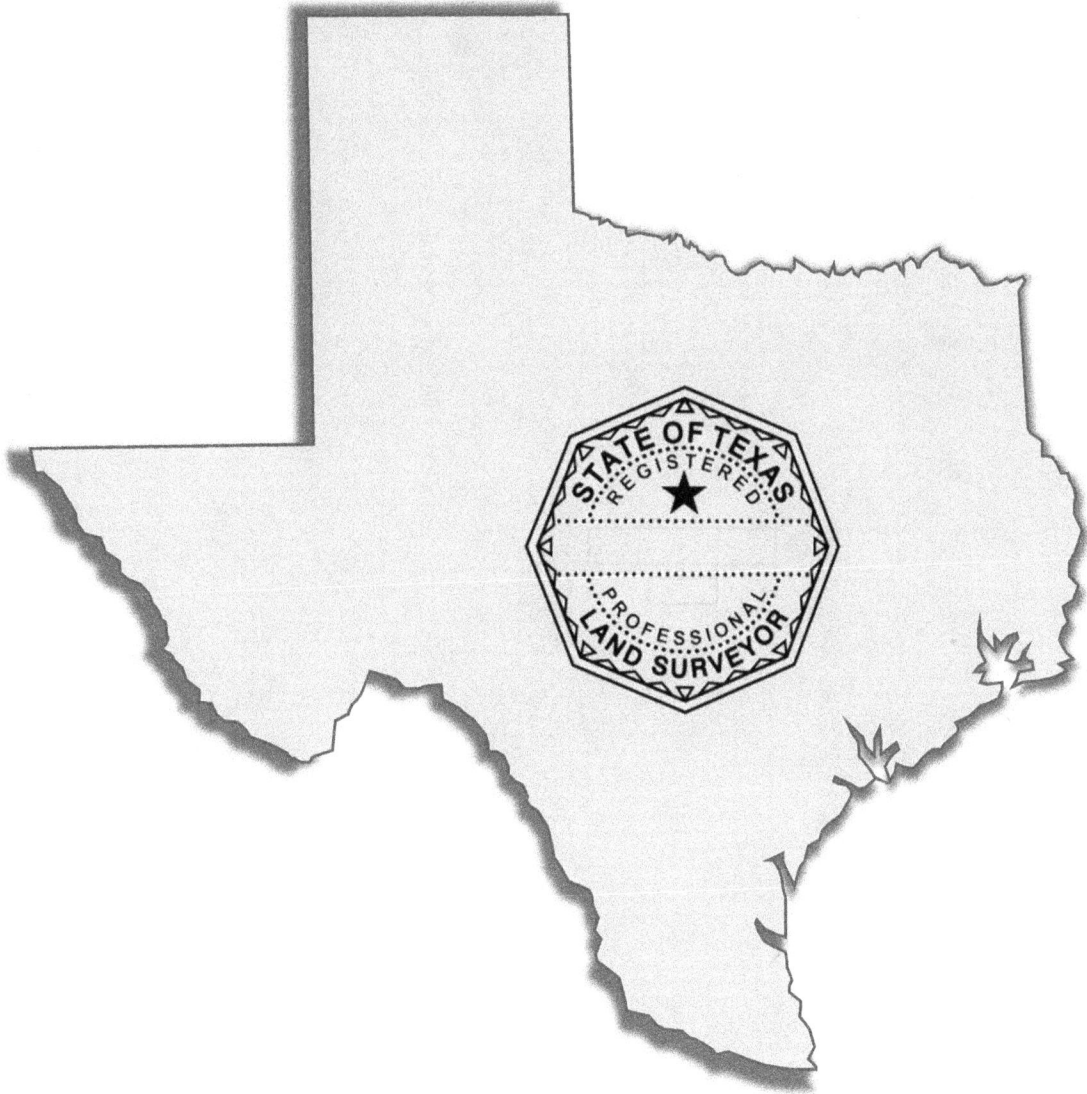

Dane M. Courville, R.P.L.S.

PREFACE

I began surveying in the State of Maine in 2005. On day one, I knew I was a surveyor at heart. The job and all it entails was a perfect fit for me and my life. The ability to be outside, perform historical research, performing mathematical computations, meeting landowners, learning to identify trees, cutting line, investigating and assisting with legal matters, and learning new equipment and technology, all seemed to be right up my alley. I graduated from the University of Louisiana at Lafayette with a degree in Biological Anthropology with a focus on forensic and biological sciences. After graduation I became a licensed elementary Montessori teacher and taught for a year in Sugar Land, Texas. Following teaching, I volunteered for a summer in Ely, Nevada and Grangeville, Idaho with the Bureau of Land Management. My volunteer efforts quickly turned into a full time job, and I stayed in central Nevada for a few years. With the Bureau of Land Management I was performing archaeological duties and working with the recreational department mapping archaeological sites and trails. I learned how to use mapping and survey equipment throughout the process. After departing Nevada for a move to Maine in 2005, I found employment with Ginn Land Surveying and Plisga and Day Land Surveyors in Bangor, Maine. With these firms I gained a tremendous amount of surveying knowledge and a skill set that put me on course to becoming licensed. I became licensed in the State of Maine in 2007 as a Land Surveyor in Training (LSIT) and finally a Professional Land Surveyor (PLS) in 2009. Leaving Maine lead me back to Texas where I gained my Registered Professional Land Surveyor (RPLS) in 2010. I transferred to Colorado in 2015, and subsequently obtained my professional land surveyor licenses in Vermont, Colorado, and Oregon. In all, I have gained 15 years of survey experience working in many different survey disciplines (e.g. residential, commerical, ALTA, energy sector, transportation, construction, etc.).

An essential part of studying for the Texas Registered Professional Land Surveyor (RPLS) examination is getting your hands on, reading, and comprehending the information presented in the text "*Selected Texas Statutes and Boundary Decisions for Land Surveyors, Land Title Agents, and Title Attorneys*" by Kenneth G. Gold a Registered Professional Land Surveyor. This text is considered a must have by many licensed surveyors in the State of Texas. While studying for the state specific examination I read, re-read, and re-read again Kenneth Gold's book. During several of these readings, I began to take meticulous notes and wrote short cut or brief descriptions of what I deemed to be the critical and fundamental elements of the text. The following guide is the compilation of those notes as well as other relevant surveying knowledge. I hope that the guide herein will serve as an assistant while reading the book yourself. I would not recommend substituting the original book with this condensed and simplified guide, but rather making it a supplement.

I wish you the very best on your journey to becoming a Texas RPLS. Enjoy the path forward and remember to learn from it.

If you have any questions or concerns regarding the material presented in this manual, feel free to reach out to me at surveyingmanual@gmail.com.

Thanks for your support,

TABLE OF CONTENT

GENERAL TIMELINE OF TEXAS SOVEREIGNTY

Texas history is a tumultuous story of exploration, imperialism, battles and war, independence, and allegiance. The "Six Flags of Texas" represents the six separate sovereignties that ruled and/or governed the lands that encompass the State of Texas throughout history. The general timeline of these entities are as follows:

SPAIN	1519-1685 (Spanish initial exploration/claim of the region)
FRANCE	1685-1689 (sporadic and brief, no grants were established)
SPAIN	1690-1821
MEXICO	1821-1836
REPUBLIC OF TEXAS	1836-1845
UNITED STATES	1845-1860 (statehood gained on December 29, 1845)
CONFEDERACY	1861-1865 (the period during the Civil War Era)
UNITED STATES	1865- present

HISTORY OF TEXAS

Line of demarcation (1493)

The line of demarcation was first established 100 leagues west of the Azores and Cape Verde Islands. It was defined by Pope Alexander VI. It was stated that lands west of the line were to be controlled by Spain and lands east of the line were to be controlled by Portugal.

Treaty of Tordesillas (June 7, 1494)

The original line of demarcation was moved 370 leagues westward. Now, everything east of the new line was in possession of Portugal and lands west of the new line were in the possession of Spain.

Alonso Alvarez de Pineda (1520)

Pineda was the first European to "see" Texas. Saw it from a sailing vessel while mapping the Gulf of Mexico coastline. He was leading an expedition requested by the governor of Jamaica, Francisco de Garay, to discover a passageway from the Gulf of Mexico to Asia.

Alvar Nunez Cabeza de Vaca and the Narvaez expedition (1528-1535)

Nunez was the first European to "touch" Texas. He was ship wrecked near Galveston and was subsequently enslaved by natives living in the area. After his enslavement, he further explored the interior of the area now designated as Texas.

Rene-Robert Cavelier Sieur de la Salle (1684-1687)

Spain essentially ignored the lands it staked claim to from the Pineda expedition for nearly 160 years. Towards the end of this period, France attempted to claim the Mississippi River Valley in an effort to separate Florida from Spain. La Salle was sent by King Louis XIV to stake claim to the valley. By a grievous mis-calculation, La Salle settled in Matagorda Bay. La Salle attempted to correct the mistake and searched by sea and land for the Mississippi River failing each time. During the colonization attempt, they did create Fort Saint Louis; however, no land grants were recorded. La Salle and the residents of Fort Saint Louis were eventually killed by Spanish expeditions sent to remove the French.

Captain Alonzo de Leon (1690)

Leon was sent by Spain via Mexico City to evict La Salle. During this effort, he explored and mapped interior Texas and named several rivers including San Marcos, Guadalupe, Medina, Nueces, and the Trinity Rivers. After finding Fort Louis nearly abandoned by La Salle, Leon established a Mission in East Texas called the Mission San Francisco de los Tejos.

Spanish government land grants to missions (1690-1716)

A major push by Spain to expand the reach of Christianity resulted in the establishment of several missions throughout Texas. Three of the original missions were as follows: La Espada (1690), Conception (1716), and San Juan (1716).

Nacogdoches mission (1716)

The establishment these missions would produce trails from Mexico to Louisiana. This system of roads/trails were the Camino Real (The Royal Road or the Kings Highway) and the Old San Antonio Road between the Rio Grande and the Sabine Rivers. One of the major stations along the road was the Nacogdoches mission.

Don Juan Antonio Perez de Almazan (1731)

Almazan was the captain of the San Antonio de Bexar Presidio. He order for the first survey of the town of San Antonio. Town Lots were subsequently granted to Canary Islanders.

Grants to 40 native tribes (1731-1745)

The establishment of missions throughout Texas in an effort to convert and baptize native communities into Christianity, 40 Indian tribes were awarded land grants.

Spanish Royal Commission arrives (1767)

The Commission finally arrives to establish surveying standards and forms the basis of establishing settlement areas. The settlers of Jose de Escandon in South Texas requested land surveys as early as 1753.

Ordenanza de Intendentes (December 4, 1786)

An Intendente was an individual of judicial, military, and/or administrative authority of a given district or administrative unit. Large regions were further divided into smaller districts, and each of these districts were governed by an Intendente. The order of 1786 stated these Intendentes were permitted to grant land.

Louisiana Purchase (1803)

The United States under the presidency of Thomas Jefferson purchased the Louisiana Territory encompassing 828,000 square miles from France. The western line of the territory was in dispute prior to the purchase between France and Spain, and continued after the purchase between the United States and Spain.

Eastern boundary of Texas established (1805)

A Spanish Royal Decree set the boundary between the United States and Texas as the Nueces River.

Filibusters (1812-1813)

In 1810 and 1811, revolts in Mexico and Texas began the fight for Mexican independence from Spain. These revolts eventually began the Mexican War of Independence. The Texan/Mexican rebels sought support from follow Mexicans, Americans, French, and Natives. Representatives sought official support from Washington DC and were rejected. These forces opt for a filibuster approach (unauthorized military action into foreign lands aimed at revolution or secession), making Texas a free and independent state within the Spanish territory.

Adams-Onis Treaty (1819)

A Spanish negotiator deals with the United States and re-establishes the United States-Spanish boundary to be the Sabine River. The west line of the Louisiana Territory is ultimately determined.

Mexican independence from Spain (1821)

Mexico began the fight for independence from Spain in 1810. Not until 1821 did, Mexico finally became an independent nation.

Empresarios (1821)

An empresario was a land contractor within a colonization system established by the Mexican government. The first empresario, Moses Austin, and his son Stephen F. Austin, were granted permission from the Spanish/Mexican government to settle three hundred families.

First United States attempt to purchase Texas from Mexico (1822-1827)

John Quincy Adams, the then United States president, offered Mexico $1 million for the purchase of Texas.

Second United States attempt to purchase Texas from Mexico (1829)

Andrew Jackson, the then United States president, offered Mexico $5 million for the purchase of Texas.

Mexican Federal Act of May 7, 1824

The Mexican government combines the individual Mexican states of Coahulia and Texas.

Mexican Law of April 6, 1830

The Law was enacted to attempt to stop the immigration of United State citizens into the Mexican region of Texas. The Law focused on making sure empresarios were adhering to colonization laws and suspended many existing empresario contracts.

Republic of Texas is formed (May 14, 1836)

Santa Anna giving Texas its independence from Mexico by signing the Republic of Texas treaty.

Texas independence (March 1836)

Stephen F. Austin becomes the first elected president of the Republic of Texas. Houston is founded in 1836 as the Capitol. (Andrew Jackson was the current United States president).

Act of December 19, 1836

Defines Texas Boundary as:

Lands north and east of the Rio Grande up to the river's source, thence north to the 46th latitude, thence with the treaty boundary of Spain and the United States set in 1805. The newly formed Texas Congress set the southern boundary of the Republic as the Rio Grande in spite of the Mexican government not recognizing Texas independence.

General Land Office (GLO) established (December 22, 1836)

In 1836, the Republic of Texas Congress created the General Land Office to manage the Republic's public lands. The purpose of the General Land Office was to collect land records and maps of Mexican and Spanish land grant records, to assist in settling land disputes associated with public lands, and ultimately to assist in the settlement of the Republic's public lands. First commissioner was John Petit Borden 1836-1840. A total of eleven office headquarters were established.

Act of March 16, 1840

Texas officially adopts Common Law as the "Law of the Land".

Texas annexation (1845-1846)

February 1844 the United States congress, under the presidency of James Polk, passed a congressional joint resolution stating if Texas agrees to three conditions it would become a state. The conditions were as follows:

1) All owed funds and debts shall be retained by the Republic of Texas.
2) All undivided/owed lands within the Republic of Texas be sold, and the earnings are applied to the Republic's debt.
3) Any lands, after the Republic's debts are paid, cannot be given to the United States as a charge.

As a result, on December 1844, the Texas constitution was drafted and accepted by the United States congress and statehood was obtained.

February 19, 1845

United States of America flag was adopted in the State Capital in Austin, Texas. Texas obtains its statehood.

Mexican War (July 1845 to February 1848)

After the 1845 annexation of Texas by the United States, a war with Mexico began. Mexico considered Texas as part of its Mexican territory and did not agree with the annexation. Texas and United State forces set out to defend its land up north of the Rio Grande. Zachary Taylor was deployed as the war general by James Polk, the current United States president.

Confirmation of Mexican/Spanish land titles (February 10, 1852)

After the Mexican War 234 Mexican and Spanish land grants were left unresolved and unconfirmed due to the change of control of Texas from Mexico to the United States annexed State of Texas. The legislative confirmation act of 1852 allowed for the confirmation and validation of these land grants per the General Land Office's recommendation.

Texas is shaped over time as follows:

East boundary - center of Sabine River up to 32 degrees North Latitude (1848)
West boundary - sold off all lands to the north and New Mexico to the United States
          (Compromise of 1850)
North boundary - south bank of the Red River with Oklahoma (1921-1923)
South boundary - deepest channel of the Rio Grande from the Gulf of Mexico to the
          southern boundary of New Mexico (Treaty of Guadalupe-Hildalgo 1848)

TITLE

Grantor vs. Grantee
Grantor=seller and Grantee=buyer

Real property interests
Possessory

Fee simple absolute - no encumbrances or stipulations.

Fee simple defeasible - voided on certain expressed conditions.

Fee simple conditional - grantee must produce heir.

Fee tail - may only pass to grantee's heir(s).

Estate of life - use during grantee's natural life only.

Non-Possessory

Easement - right to use another's land.

Covenant - a promise concerning land.

License - a privilege to use another's land.

Profit a Pendre - right to remove material.

Emblements - use and profit of crops.

Encumbrances
Mortgage - debt in association to property and title.

Lien - the right to keep possession of property until a debt compensated.

Tax lien - non-payment of taxes.

Mechanics lien - non-payment of services.

Statutory lien - lien placed by statute(s).

Methods of transfer
Written - through a deed, will, patent, or eminent domain.

Unwritten - adverse possession, implied dedication, waiver, practical location, unwritten agreement, estoppel, acquiescence, nature. Unwritten rights become senior to written rights.

UNWRITTEN RIGHTS OF LAND

Surveyor responsibilities

A surveyor should always show and document both record lines and occupation lines, whether coinciding or different.

A surveyor's task is to determine boundary location based on evidence and fact according to the written record documents, it is not to determine of ownership. Ownership is a legal issue.

Terms

Possessor - party or parties to which current ownership/title is granted. The individual(s) of record ownership.

Claimant - party or parties attempting to obtain ownership/title. The individual(s) not of record ownership.

Adverse possession

The occupation of land titled to another with the intention of gaining possession of said land. A surveyor's role in determining adverse possession is as follows: first, recommend the client to seek counsel regarding adverse possession. Second, know the elements of adverse possession. Finally, identify and detail the area of possession and conflicting area of occupation.

Elements of adverse possession
1) Intent - the claimant of adverse possession must show true intent of possession (i.e., merely the construction of a fence is not sufficient).
2) Actual - the occupation of land in question must be "visible in nature".
3) Open - the use and intent of the land in question is made aware to possessor and the public in general.
4) Hostile (adverse) - the possessor and the claimant have opposing and inconsistent views of land ownership.
5) Time statutes
   - 3 years - possessor must recover the land in question within a 3-year period from opposing possession by a claimant to restart clock.
   - 5 years - possessor must recover the land in question within a 5-year period opposing possession by a claimant if the claimant is a) currently using the land, b) paying taxes on the land, and c) has a duly registered deed.

- 10 years - possessor must recover the land in question within a 10-year period from opposing possession by a claimant if the claimer is a) currently using the land, b) has no title instrument to the land in question that is less than 160 acres, and c) has a duly registered deed.
- 25 years - possessor must recover the land in question within a 25 year period given the possessor is disabled (overall adverse possession time requirement).
- Tacking - current claimant uses the time accumulated from previous claimants for use towards meeting a time limit requirement.

6) Color of Title - possessor must have TRUE title of the land in question. Color of title provides for the appearance of "good and valid" title, but in actuality, the title is not valid.
7) Peaceable - the occupation by the claimant must be continuous and uninterrupted.
8) Non-disabled owner - the possessor must be at least 18 years of age, "sane", and not in the military during war.
9) Non-Public land - the land in question must not be of public domain. Adverse possession of public land is not permitted by statute.

Burdens of adverse possession claim

1) The burden to prove adverse possession is on the claimant and not the possessor/record owner.
2) Evidence must be clear and convincing.
3) Possessor must rely on the strength of their possession as opposed to the weakness of the record owner's title.
4) Defendant (record owner) has to prove the possessor had permission.

Prescriptive easement

The main difference between adverse possession and prescriptive easements is that adverse possession is associated with fee simple title (resulting in possession) and prescriptive easement claims will never develop into a fee simple title (result in right of use only).

As with adverse possession, the main responsibility of a surveyor regarding prescriptive easement claims is to identify the areas of uses, not to determine of ownership or possession rights.

Elements of prescriptive easement

1) Open & Notorious - notification to owner, not secretive.
2) Location - bounds of use are definable and remain the same.
3) Continuous - constant, uninterrupted use.
4) Exclusive - individual use, not even the owner can use the easement area.
5) Adverse - without permission by possessor.

6) Time duration requirement - **10 years** of continuous, non-occasional use; the 3, 5, 10, and 25 years statutes dealing with adverse possession are held inapplicable to the creation of prescriptive easements in Texas.

Agreement & Acquiescence

Acquiescence - the main element of Acquiescence is uncertainty, doubt, and/or dispute. If the true line location is known, acquiescence to a line is not possible. The time duration requirement is sometime AFTER adverse possession's statutes of limitations (between 25 years; possibly 10 years). Acquiescence can be summarized as the SILENT assumption of a line's location between two parties

Agreement - verbal, parol, oral agreement of a line's location between two parties. The intention of agreement is not to agree to an incorrect line location, instead an agreement is reached due to the fact the "true" line is unknown or unascertainable.

Note: Once a line's location is determined or set by acquiescence or agreement the new line holds and the previous "unknown line" location is void.

Estoppel

The lawful protection of landowners from another landowner's allegations or denials of a fact that contradicts their own previous acts. Good Faith reliance on the words and/or actions of another causes the expense of time, money, and effort to be lost if the words and actions are found to be untrue. The lawful protection of a landowner from another landowner's allegations or denials of a fact(s) that contradicts their own previous acts.

Example of estoppel
    A farmer is told by his neighbor "the field on the top of the hill is definitely yours", so the farmer constructs a barn in the field on the top of the hill. Later the field on the top of the hill is found be owned by neighbor. The farmer is not responsible for the loss of land the neighbor mistakenly granted to the farmer with the purpose of housing a barn.

Elements of estoppel
    1) One puts forth omissions, declaration, words, actions, etc.
    2) One's omissions, words, actions, etc. cause reasonable and foreseeable reliance by another.
    3) Expenditures otherwise would not have been made having known the truth.
    4) Expenditures cause injury or loss.

Nature

Erosion and avulsion of land can cause change in title when dealing with riparian lands (refer to section on riparian and littoral rights).

Common reputation

Common reputation is long, continuous, recognition from "uninvolved" yet knowledgeable persons is used to determine boundary. LAST CASE RESORT for line determination and is only used if evidence, witness testimony, etc. have disappeared or are unascertainable.

Practical location

True location is not known, but the location is "believed" to be known.

Practical location is when a common grantor or two parties agree and monument a common boundary. After the agreement between involved parties, any inaccuracies of said line are considered finalized and resolved. There are no further disputes (unlike in an agreement).

Elements of practical location:
1) Original boundary is vague and truly unknown.
2) The newly decided line must be monumented.

SURVEYING AND TEXAS LAW

What (law) vs. where (survey)

What lines are is a matter of law.

Where lines are is a matter of survey.

Example

An iron pin is found during a survey.

Survey perspective - is the iron pin the iron pin called for in the deed? The interpretation of evidence by the surveyor is the basis of this opinion. The question the surveyor must ask is does the iron pin found represent the iron pin called for in the deed, and WHERE is the corner because of this determination?

Law perspective - the pin is the property corner. The law comes into play in this situation in determining WHAT the iron pin represents. Yes, the surveyor claims it is the iron pin called for in the deed, and the iron pin determines the location of the corner per deed, but law determines if it is the property corner.

Lawsuit types

Boundary dispute - it is the plaintiff's responsibility show a preponderance of evidence of a contested boundary line on the ground.

Trespass to try title - the attempt to recover land that has been lawfully withheld from the true landowner.

The most important objectives in a boundary or trespass to try title suit are
1) Find intent of parties.
2) Follow the "footsteps" of the original survey.

The test to determine whether a trespass to try title suit is really a boundary dispute is:
If there would have been no case if not for the question of boundary, then the case is a boundary suit even though it might involve questions of title.

Law origins

(King's Law) PRIOR to 1840 (Civil Law) - basis for Spanish and Mexican land grants and colonization.

AFTER March 1840 (Common Law) - established through court rulings and precedence.

Note: There is a brief period between the Republic of Texas gaining its independence from Mexico and it adopting common law (law of courts). During this period, the Republic of Texas had its independence and still maintained the Mexican/Spanish civil law (law of kings) rules. The duration was approximately four years.

EVIDENCE

Burden of proof

The plaintiff has the burden of proof.
The defendant has burden of being present once plaintiff has met the burden of proof.

With <u>criminal</u> cases the burden is "<u>beyond reasonable doubt</u>"
(scales of justice are tipped ALL the way; must be a 100% to 0% favor).

With <u>boundary</u> cases the burden is "<u>preponderance of evidence</u>"
(scales of justice are tipped slightly; has to be at least a 51% to 49% favor).

Evidence as it pertains to records and documents

- A deed is evidence of title but not proof of title. The deed can serve in the assistance to establish title only.
- That which is clear cannot be made unclear by the addition of uncalled for evidence. If the record speaks for itself, then additional evidence should not, and cannot, be introduced. This is also known as the "Four Corners Rule": The document/deed should have everything needed to make a determination; one should not have to look any further than the "four corners" of the document/deed (see section on "four corners rule" below).
- Parol (verbal) evidence can never dispute written evidence. Written evidence takes precedence over parol evidence.
- The document/deed should be reviewed in its entirety and not "pieced out". The document/deed as a whole should be considered as it relates to its complete self. One cannot excerpt out parts without consideration of all the parts.
- The description should identify the property and not "define" the property. Location, location, location; not characteristics.
- External documents referenced inside a subject deed/document hold just as much weight as the subject deed itself. Simple reference to or mention of other documents within a subject deed allows for the use of said referenced documents.
- Extrinsic evidence can only be used to clarify that which is unclear. If the deed/document is clear and the intent is outlined, then extrinsic evidence cannot be used.

Types of evidence
- Parol/evidence aliunde - verbal/oral testimony can only be used to clarify an ambiguity. If intent is known, then parol evidence may not be used. Typically, verbal testimony is provided by an unbiased, third party that will not be affected by the result of the testimony. It is used only to support only found evidence.
- Hearsay - a statement provided in court that was initially made outside of the court.
- Common report - that which is known and accepted by several individuals (common knowledge).

Regarding the above evidence, the following must be implied:
- Can only provide evidence of title, but not title itself.
- Is utilized as a "last case resort".
- Cannot contradict valid written evidence.
- Individual(s) providing the evidence are considered unbiased.

Primary duty of a surveyor
Intent is discovered through evidence. Revealing the intent is paramount and is the most important aspect of survey boundary determination/analysis.

The surveyor needs to understand that ONLY the facts should apply to boundary determination, the intent is revealed through the facts and documentation left by the original survey. Remember, what the original surveyor did and what he/she imagined (wanted to do) are two separate things. In other words, a surveyor is not in the business of figuring out what was wanted or assumed, but rather what is stated and/or written.

Finding intent
1) Follow <u>footsteps</u> of the original surveyor- line monumentation is equally as crucial as corner monumentation; courts expect the lines to be "run".
2) Use of and knowledge of <u>rules or construction/dignity of calls</u>.
3) Application of <u>junior and senior rights</u>.
4) Find and use <u>best possible evidence</u>.

Extrinsic evidence
Extrinsic evidence is evidence that is made available from outside the written document/deed.

Extrinsic evidence is used to clarify intent. It helps determine location, but it will never change location. As with parol, hearsay, and common report, extrinsic evidence must only be used as a "last case resort".

Uses for extrinsic evidence may include
- Verification of monumentation or location.
- Clarification of errors, omissions, and conflict.
- Definition or term identification.
- Validation or proof of lost documents/deeds.
- Clarification of ambiguities.

> Types of ambiguities
>> Latent - less obvious; not on the face of the deed. The language is clear and decisive, but application of outside evidence creates doubt or multiple meanings.
>>> (e.g., the ambiguity is revealed when the deed wording is compared to the real situation in the field).
>> Patent - obvious; on the face of the deed. The language is unclear and indecisive.
>>> (e.g., *North 33 degrees 25 seconds **North**, a distance of 223.65 feet*; is obviously incorrect).

> Note: When ambiguities arise, the grantee is given favor over the grantor. It is assumed the grantor's responsibility to construct a clear land description.

What can be used as extrinsic evidence:
- Parol evidence.
- Photos.
- Unrecorded documents/papers.
- Contemporaneous or subsequent acts.
- Declarations of knowledge.

Four corners rule

The four corners rule is the concept of determining the intentions of the parties from the language in the deed and the deed only; not using extrinsic or extraneous evidence if possible. The idea is if one holds the deed by the four corners and they need not look any further for information.

Extraneous evidence

Evidence referenced within the subject of the deed/documentation. Referenced items become just as relevant as the subject documentation itself.

Best Evidence

The best evidence is that which is ascertainable from the original survey. However, the lowest degree of evidence can and will be admissible by the court to determine boundary if it is the only and best possible/available evidence.

RULES OF CONSTRUCTION/DIGNITY OF CALLS

Texas dignity of calls

Each element of a survey utilized in the interpretation and analysis of boundaries are ordered hieratically. The prioritization of these elements is as follows:

1) Documented/recorded and field book notated lines and corners marked by the original surveyor are paramount.
2) Natural monuments (e.g., stone, tree, river, etc.).
3) Artificial Monuments (e.g., fence post, rebar, bolt, etc.).
   > Note: Marked natural monuments become artificial monuments in dignity. (e.g., blazed tree, craved stone, etc.).
4) Adjoiner
   A call for an adjoiner can be natural or artificial depending on the type of monument used to mark the adjoiner's boundary perimeter at the time of the documentation. These objects/monuments must exist and be ascertained.
   > Note: If the adjoiner's line is not definable or ascertainable, course and distance hold.
   > Note: Adjoiner calls are essentially equal to the natural and/or artificial monuments used to mark the lines.
5) Courses (bearings).
6) Distances (lengths).
7) Quantity (area).

Junior vs senior rights

Senior Rights - holds over junior rights.
Junior Rights - gives way to senior rights.
Equal Rights - found in simultaneous conveyances (e.g., subdivisions).

"Superiority" determination of dates

1) Date of survey.
2) Original field note date.
3) Patent description date.

Order of precedence to consider

1) Intent.
2) Original location.
3) Monuments (called for in operative record).
   > Note: Operative record is that which creates the line; the monuments represent the original line.
4) Measurements.
5) Area.

Intent

Intent is the true meaning as derived from the wording of the document/deed. Intent requires no interpretation; the meaning should be obvious and have no ambiguity. If intent is known and understood clearly then GO NO FURTHER with the rules of construction, there is no need to construct anything.

In the writing of a deed, it is the responsibility of the grantor to lay out intent. If ambiguity does arise, then favor will be given to the grantee in any interpretations.

Obvious: Do NOT apply rules of construction.
Unobvious: Apply rules of construction.

Original location

Original location is the location of the boundary at the time of its creation. All the evidence, monuments, etc. are simply there to help determine and indicate this original location. The evidence does not hold, the line holds. There is a difference between a corner and a monument. The monument physically indicates the actual corner, but it is not the corner. The monument marks the corner as evidence marks the lines.

Monuments

Types of monumentation

Material

- Natural - hold the highest priority (e.g. tree).
- Artificial - hold the second highest priority (e.g., 5/8" iron rebar and cap).
- Record - priority is variable depending on whether natural or artificial, monumentation is used to mark the lines and corners of said record calls.

Recorded vs. unrecorded

- Documented - hold the highest priority; these monuments are called for in the operative record.
- Undocumented - hold the second highest priority; these are not called for in the operative record.
- Possession - hold the least priority (e.g. uncalled evidence of occupation, such as a fence along a property line).

Condition
- Existent - the monument is present and represents the corner, corner location is determined by an original or approved replacement monument, or through accepted accessories to original or replacement monument.
- Disturbed - monument is existent, but visibly disturbed.
- Obliterated - corner location is not available, but can be restored through: a) competent testimony, b) accepted record evidence, c) improvements built at the time the original position was known, and/or d) a monument proven to be the replacement of the original corner.
- Lost corner - corner location that is not available and cannot be determined based on evidence. A lost corner requires mathematical analysis from other found corners for repositioning. Lost corners are the only corners requiring mathematical computation.

Rights status
- Senior - the monument is called for in earlier or original records.
- Junior - the monument is called for in later or subsequent records.

Order of precedence with monumentation evidence
1) Original monument.
2) Subsequent "chain of evidence" monument.
3) Witness monument.

Note: If monuments are not called for in the document/deed, then they simply become supplemental evidence.

Ways monumentation can represent a corner
- Locative - the monument representing a corner (e.g. *to a pin*).
- Witness/reference tie - the monument holds a position from which the corner location can be derived (e.g. *to a rebar, from which the SE corner bears North 50 feet*).
- Passing - the monument holds the line between the corners (e.g. *passing a tree stump and continuing on said course to….*).

Locative vs. descriptive
Given the following example: *Thence to a stone in a fence line.*
- The call is to the STONE and is the locative call.
- The call is descriptive in mentioning the fence line, but the FENCE LINE is descriptive; not the call.

Rules of monumentation
1) A called for monument is calling for the position the monument marks, not the monument itself. This is the corner vs. monument difference; the monument represents/marks the corner and is not the corner itself.

2) Precedence - first and most superior, an original monument holds. Second, a replacement, "chain of evidence" monument holds. Third and last, a witness monument hold.
3) Monuments are controlling only if they are:
    a. Called for in operative document.
    b. In the same position (undisturbed).
    c. Set in the condition as called for in the cited conveyance.
    d. Existent at the time of the conveyance.
4) Due to assumption of impartiality, public sector surveyor monumentation is consider higher in priority than private sector surveyor monumentation.
5) Priority
    a. Natural over artificial monuments.
    b. Called for over uncalled for monuments.
    c. Locative over passing.
        i. Witness monuments called for in writing have the same weight as an unfound corner monument.
        ii. Witness monuments help locate corner monuments and do not substitute for them.
        iii. Passing monuments hold little weight.
        iv. Witness monuments can help find corner monuments, but do not refute a found, original, and undisturbed corner monument.
    d. Documented over undocumented over possession, but undocumented and possession monuments can assist in locating a corner.
    e. Locative over descriptive.

Exceptions/Caveats to the rules of monumentation
- Disturbed monumentation loses all or some validity.
- Monuments will not hold if the grantor's intent clearly states otherwise in the written record.
- If the found monument is clearly a mistake it will not hold.
- Regarding senior title dispute, a monument will not extend a parcel's coverage beyond its entitlement.

Ways to identify monumentation
- Time.
- Physical characteristics.
- Markings.
- Relation to other markings.
- Public or private records.
- Parol evidence.
- Hearsay evidence.
- Common report.
- Measurements from other accepted monumentation.
- Witness or reference tie monumentation.
- Trees.

Measurements

Rules for distances and direction (measurements)

- The most certain rules.
- Measurements only assist in locating monuments.
- When in doubt, direction is assumed to be magnetic (in public lands states, the assumption is true north).
- Directions and distances are to be run in the original order of establishment.
- Direction over distance (in public lands states where distance is over direction).
- Distances are assumed to be ground distances.

Areas

Area calls are considered with the least weight and are utilized if no other element of construction is available.

ROADS AND TRAVELED WAYS

Centerline of road assumptions

It is assumed that fee title/ownership extends to the centerline of the traveled way unless the conveyance expresses clear reservations pertaining to the right-of-way limits. Additionally, the public has assumed access to right-of-way limits.

This presumption exists regardless of whether or not the description (metes and bounds) around the parcel excludes the area to the centerline. Just because the deed calls do not go to the centerline of the traveled way and terminate at the right-of-way limits does not mean title does not extend to the centerline.

The presumption does not apply if:
      1) The grantor owns both sides of the right-of-way.
      2) The right-of-way is larger or more valuable than the land being conveyed.

The construction of a new roadway entirely encompassed on a parcel of land does NOT necessarily give title to the centerline of said roadway for a parcel adjacent to the newly constructed roadway. Title of the roadway will not extend to the centerline of the roadway for any later divided off parcels from the adjacent lands (see depiction below).

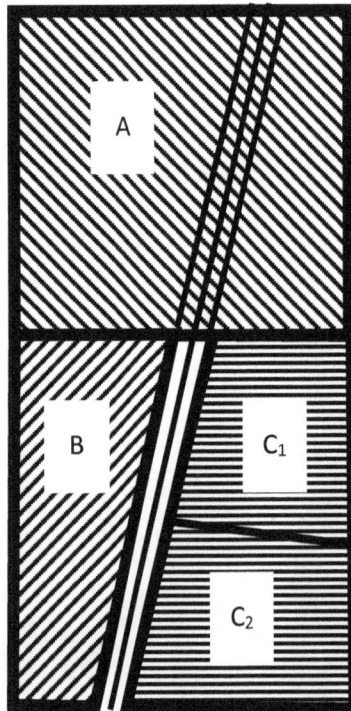

Title to centerline of roadway through parcel A does not necessarily translate to title being to centerline of the roadway as it runs along parcels B and C. Title can "zigzag" between right-of-way limit and centerline from parcel to adjoining parcel depending on the verbiage in the conveyance documents associated with each individual parcel.

C was divided later into parcels C_1 and C_2, but title still does not extend to centerline.

Dedication

Landowner sets apart/grants land for public use.

The elements of dedication are as follows:
1) Dedicator must actually own the land.
2) Dedicator makes an expressed (written or stated) or implied offer.
3) Implied - not written or stated but the landowner intentions are clear and unequivocal such as follows:
   a.   Owners performed clear act showing intent to dedicate.
   b.   Dedicator is competent.
   c.   The public uses the dedicated lands.
   d.   There was an offer and acceptance.
4) Dedication serves the public in a useful manner.
5) Dedication is accepted.

Claims of "not found" vs. "not recorded"

When labeling roadways on plats or in deed descriptions it is a good idea and good practice to claim the roadway as "records NOT FOUND" rather than "records UNRECORDED". A surveyor is better off claiming they did not find the record rather than making the assumption the record of the roadway was never recorded. This same concept applies with other encumbrances associated with a parcel of land being surveyed (e.g., easements).

Term use of "right-of-way"

Simply stating in the description the term "right-of-way" as the intended use of the roadway does NOT necessarily make the use of the roadway an easement. It still has the potential to be a fee title conveyance. The "right-of-way" phrase could merely be intending the type of use on the land being conveyed as fee title. The "right-of-way" phrase is not a fail-safe term to be use for a roadway easement.

Railroad right-of-ways

Similarly, as with roadways or traveled ways, railroad conveyances are to centerline unless clear, expressive intent is shown otherwise in the language of the conveyance. A deed description to "edge", "side", etc. of the right-of-way does NOT show clear, expressive intent (same as roadway assumptions). The purpose of this assumption is that historically many more easement grants were made compared to fee title grants for railways. It is not good practice to use existing rails to calculate the centerline to tie-off limits of railroad right-of-way. Like a traveled way the centerline of the road/rail and the centerline of the associated easement may be two separate lines. Though it is not recommended, there are times where the existing rails are the best evidence available to recreate the railroad right-of-way.

Abandonment

The requirement for abandonment of a traveled way is as follows: enclosure of an infrequently used roadway by one or more property owners with a fence showing intent of non-use continuously for a 20-year period. Non-use alone does not suffice.

After the enactment of abandonment by meeting all requirements, the abutting landowners gain vesting title to the centerline of the roadway. In other words, the traveled way's previously designated area is divided evenly between the abutting landowners on each side. Note: If the traveled way is entirely encompassed by a single landowner, then the said landowner is provided all lands previously designated by the traveled way.

Land locked land transportation code

The owner of a land locked parcel of land can fill out an application with the state claiming the "how, where, and why" of the situation. Once the application is filled and processed, a court appointed Jury of View made of five property owners work with a county surveyor to plan an access road to the land locked parcel. The road that is most "advantageous" to the public will be validated and implemented.

Methods to best locate an existing highway right-of-way will involve research of the following:

- Age of the highway.
- Quality or detail of alignment maps.
- Explicitness or thoroughness of acquisition descriptions.
- Type of taking.
- Existence of monumentation.
- Recovery of the road base or centerline.

EASEMENTS

Definition

Easement - a privilege, service, or convenience a party is authorized to use within the property of another.

According to *Brown's Boundary Control and Legal Principles* an easement is defined as: "An Interest in land created by grant or agreement that confers a right upon owners to some profit, benefit, dominion, or lawful use of or over the estate of another; it is distinct from ownership of soil."

Easements: <u>Rights</u> are granted **NOT** <u>Title.</u>

Easement documentation should state LOCATION and PURPOSE

> Example: "Over the lands of Smith for horse cart transportation".

Conveyance of fee or easement

Main elements of a conveyance (either fee or easement) are as follows:
1) Written out and expressed.
2) Names of grantor and grantee or provided.
3) Sufficient description of the land being conveyed (main goal of surveyor).

The granting clause is of primary consideration, it is the essence of the conveyance, for it controls all. The granting clause can also be called the "words of conveyance". The granting clause states what is being conveyed from the grantor (the current owner) to the grantee (the purchaser).

When granting an easement, two elements in the granting clause must be stated:
1) The right.
2) The specific purpose/use of said right.

If a purpose is stated in the granting clause, it is most likely a conveyance of an easement. Without a purpose provided the conveyance most likely is that of a fee title.

Characteristics of an easement
1) An interest in land that must be created by grant or agreement, expressed or implied.
2) Interest must be on the land of another (cannot have an easement over one's own land).
3) Easement are nonpossessory; easement holder can only prevent interference with their interest.
4) Privilege to use an easement must be capable of recreation.
5) Must be described.

Types of easements

Appurtenant - attached to LAND(S); if the easement is appurtenant, it is never assumed to be in gross.

Dominant - land provided an easement (benefited from the easement).

Servient - land affected by/encumbered by an easement (burdened from the easement).

Easement in gross - attached to PERSON(S); obtained through donation, prescription, condemnation, or purchase.

Easement shapes; deficiencies and excesses

Protrusion - the easement exceeds its limits and affects the outside parcel(s).

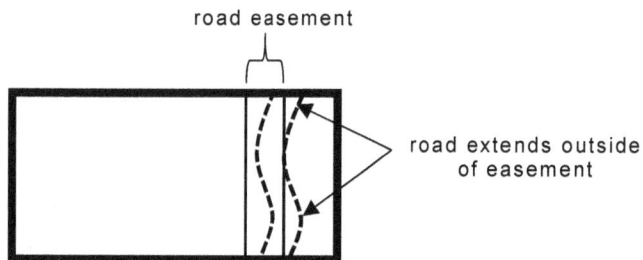

Encroachment/intrusion - the limits of the easement are crossed.

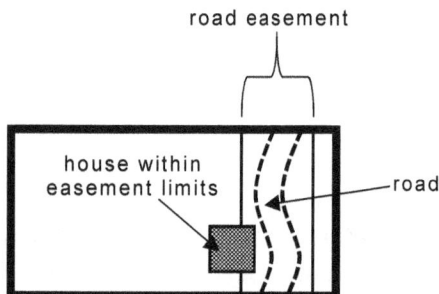

Claims of "not found" vs. "not recorded"

Easement follows the land whether or not the conveyance of said land mentions the easement. A surveyor should never make the claim they have identified all easements associated with the land, for the task of identifying all easements is nearly impossible.

It is always good practice to locate all visible utilities (along with any and all "clues" of possible hidden/invisible utility features) within the bounds and immediate vicinity of the parcel being surveyed. The field collection and subsequent noting of these features on the plat will illustrate due diligence in the identification of as many easements as possible.

Who can use the easement

Public - ALL can use.
Private - SELECTED individuals can use.

Non-use does not void an easement

Simple non-use of an easement does not warrant an easement void, invalidated, abandoned, or released.

Easement Creation

Express grant - written conveyance with description provided and stated purpose noted.

Express reservation - the easement is reserved, saved and excepted, by the grantor in a conveyance of a parcel through which the easement will exist.

Prescription - much like adverse possession, but no title is conveyed. Elements include: open, notorious, continuous for 10 years exclusively by the claimant, and adverse (see section on unwritten land rights for review).

Reference to plat - dedicatory language on a plat shows intention and grants an easement.

Negative or Positive (affirmative)

Positive - physical action on, under, or over another's land (e.g. road, well, crop, etc.).

Negative - prevention of action or use of another's land (e.g. light, air, scenic overlook, etc.).

Easement description types

Description of dominant parcel - describes the land it is going to.

Description of servient parcel - describes the land it is coming from.

Description of easement itself - describes the actual easement.

Assumption to center

It is assumed that use is to the center of an easement unless explicitly stated otherwise.

RIPARIAN AND LITTORAL LAND RIGHTS

Rights

Littoral right - right along bodies of water pertaining to shore frontages and lakes.

Riparian right - right along rivers and streams.

Changes in land/water and associated definitions

High-water line - the highest water level mark during high tide durations if tidal or typically during spring/summer months if non-tidal.

Mean high-water line - the height of water along a water body, which is the average of the higher water ranges.

Low-water line - the lowest water level mark during low tide durations if tidal or typically during fall/winter months if non-tidal.

Mean low-water line - the height of water along a water body, which is the average of the lower water ranges.

Shore - tidelands affected between mean high-water line and mean-low water line.

Bank - the line along rivers and streams at which point the vegetation line does not encroach.

Beach - the area between the mean-low water line and the line of vegetation/material change.

Thalweg - the deepest part of the deepest channel of a river or stream.

Thread - sometimes used interchangeably with the term thalweg, but in certain states it is defined as the actual middle of the river or stream being a line equidistant from each bank.

Avulsion - the sudden loss or gain of land by the action of water. Typically, land rights are not altered with a sudden change.

Erosion - the gradual loss of land by the action of water. Typically, land rights are altered with a gradual change.

Accretion - the gradual deposit and accumulation of land (sediment and deposit material known as alluvium) by the action of water. Typically, land rights are altered with a gradual change.

Alluvion/Alluvium - the actual material/soil or land that is built up and deposited during accretion.

Reliction - the <u>gradual</u> recession of water causing the exposure of previously submerged lands. Typically, land rights are altered with a gradual change.

Submergence - the <u>gradual</u> rise of water causing the covering of previously unsubmerged lands. Typically, land rights are altered with a gradual change.

Tidal cycle - the duration of time necessary to completely analyze tidal levels is 18.6 years.

Navigability

Non-navigable - not able to be sailed by ships and/or boats.
Navigable - able to be sailed by ships and/or boats.

Navigability - the average width of the stream/river, from the source to the terminus, is at least 30 feet. This width is the measurement of the bed width not simply the width of water surface. Though it is from "source to mouth", courts in the past have averaged the width along the property and near vicinity.

Another good indicator of a stream/river navigability determination is whether the land grants along the stream crossed the stream/river during their original conveyances. If they crossed, they are most likely non-navigable and if they did not cross, they are most likely navigable.

Meander lines

Meander Lines - bearing and distance calls following a watercourse whether from monument to monument on the edge of the watercourse or following the calculated centerline or waterline. These surveyor created courses are NOT the boundary. The watercourse in which the meander lines supposedly follow is the true boundary. Meander lines are not boundary lines and serve the purpose of acreage calculations. Exceptions have been made when a "substantial" amount of land remains between the meander lines and the watercourse.

Tidal boundary

Prior to 1837 (Spanish or Mexican Land Grants) - title extends to mean higher high tide which is the average of only the highest tides over a period of time.

After 1837 (Republic and State of Texas) - title extends to mean high tide which is the average of all the high tides over a period.

Open Beach Act - the public has an easement right to use the land from the low tide line upland to the vegetation line or 200 feet upland if a vegetation line does not exist. The easement is ever changing due to the changing vegetation line. This easement is along the entire Gulf of Mexico coast.

Lake boundaries

Lakes follow the same rules as streams and rivers as far as navigability, ownership, etc.

Stream boundaries

Perennial - water flows for most of a year.

Torrential - water flows less than most of the year.

State owns the "beds" of navigable streams.

State owns the "beds" of non-navigable, perennial streams/rivers if the land in which the stream/river exists were granted under the Mexican/Spanish sovereign. If the land in which the stream/river exists was granted after 1837, when the 1837 Thirty-Foot Statute passed, the streambed reverts to the adjoining landowners up to the center of the stream/river.

Centerline of a non-perennial stream is the boundary between adjoining lands.

Gradient Boundary

The gradient boundary is the line of title between State owned land and private owned land along a navigable watercourse. The bed is determined to be between the two gradient boundaries on either side of the watercourse.

The gradient boundary is determined as follows:

The line being half way between the two "qualified banks" of the accretion side of a watercourse. The higher qualified bank is determined to be the line at which the water just crests the bank. Typically, this line can be identified as the bottom of a small ditch like feature where the bank ends and the upland begins. The second qualified bank is the cut bank. This line is typically where the "steep" slope of the bank turns to a gradual slope of the river's bottom.

DEEDS

Reminder - a deed is EVIDENCE of title, but not actual TITLE.

Deed types
- Warranty - the grantor takes all the responsibility all the time.
- Special warranty/quit claim with covenants - the grantor takes responsibility only during the time of their period of ownership.
- Quit claim/release - the grantor takes no responsibility; the deed includes the statement of "I will give you everything that I was given".
- Sherriff - Like a quit claim from a county, after the statutory time period the title is guaranteed.

Deed formalities
- Must be in writing - statute of frauds.
- Must be signed by grantor - the grantee signature is optional.
- Acknowledgement - if the deed is to be used for record or authorization.
- Seals/certifications are not necessary for conveyance.
- Signature of a spouse (necessary if spouse has interest).
- Statement of consideration (how much/amount agreed on).
- Identification of grantee.
- Proper form/parts are required.

Requirements and parts of a deed
- The deed must be in writing.
- Names of both grantor and grantee/identification of parties must be provided.
- Consideration/amount must be provided.
- The deed must contain granting clause/words of conveyance.
- Operative wording must be provided.
- Adequate and locative description of property (this is main objective of surveyor) must be provided.
- Noted exceptions and reservations (as applicable) must be provided.
- Grantor's signature must be provided.
- The deed must be delivered to grantee.
- The grantee must accept of the document/deed.

Recording is not required, but always recommended

Recording of the document is not required, but if it is not it can lead to complication when seniority is to be determined.

Responsibility lies with the grantor

The grantor is responsible for the contents within the document and is responsible for the preparation of the document. Ambiguities, conflicts, etc. will be in the favor of the grantee if the intentions of the deed are unascertainable.

Responsibility of the surveyor

The surveyor is responsible for a locative and descriptive depiction of the property being conveyed. The description must be unique, from which the property is unquestionably able to be located.

Plans/plats and sketches

Plats hold over metes and bound descriptions if a conflict between the two is present. In some cases, the plat need not even be referenced in the deed document in order to hold its validity.

However; a sketch however, needs to be referenced in order to hold any legal validity. A sketch attached to a deed and not referenced can only be used to clarify ambiguities, conflicts, errors, and/or omissions from the written description.

DESCRIPTIONS

Description parts

Preamble - the generalized portion of a description.

Elements of the preamble

- County and State names.
- Original Grant Information - Abstract, Survey, etc.
- Acreage.
- Any other definitive, unique information such as land shape, address, name, etc.

Particular part - the specific and more detailed portion of the description,

This is the portion containing the specific, individual calls of the description.

Description types

- Metes and bounds - *N 22 degrees 14 minutes for 223.56 feet.*
- Plan/plat, subdivision, or referral - *Being Lot 2 of Block 1 in the Sampson Subdivision* or *Same lands described in Book 458, Page 623.*
- Bounds or adjoiner - *By and along Bear Creek* or *by and along Fredrickson.*
- Proportional/aliquot - *West half of Gaylord land* or *N/2 of the SE/4 of Section 4, T5S, R10E; 6th PM.*
- Reference to line of strip - *10 feet east and west of the herein described centerline.*
- Area/quantity - *Being 250 acres in the S/2 of Gael lands.*
- Monuments - *Billy Bob land with the set rebar* or *Along Smiths fence to a road, thence down the Bender Stream to an oak, thence up a rock wall to point of beginning.*
- Exception - *All Henderson lands except the W/2.*
- Linear - *250 feet from the west line of Drake property.*

When is a description considered sufficient

A description is considered sufficiently written when it clearly describes and identifies land for reasonable retracement by a competent surveyor.

Qualifying vs. Augmenting clauses

Qualifying - clause used for easement, exceptions, or other rights to be REMOVED from the property.

Augmentative - clause used for easement, exceptions, or other rights to be ADDED to the property.

General "etiquette" and notes

The Point of Beginning (P.O.B.) holds no more validity than any other call within a description, but it must be a record corner of the subject property being described. The point of commencement (P.O.C.) does not have to be a record corner of the subject property being described.

It is not appropriate to call for an adjoiner that is not a senior landowner.

A clockwise run description is preferable, but not always practical.

It is good practice to refer to prior recorded deed calls throughout the description. When using parenthetical statements (e.g., *N 30 29' 17" W (N 30 W)*). Remember, reference must be made to the deed being quoted in the general description.

Thumbprint syndrome - leaving a description exactly as previously written when describing a new conveyance of the same tract.

Mother Hubbard clause - a description of land that encompasses other lands not described in the description. Surveyors are not recommended to use such clauses. These clauses are known as "cover all" or "catch all" phrases describing portions of property that may have been "missed" otherwise in the description. An example of a Mother Hubbard Clause would be: "*All the lands of Tom Watts in Hidalgo County, Texas*".

APPORTIONMENTS AND
SIMULTANEOUS CONVEYANCES

Apportionment

Apportionment should only be utilized for unmarked corners between found, original monumentation. If original monuments are found at the corner in question, it will hold, and no apportionment is necessary.

When dealing with the "Texas Abstract Block Systems," generally created for massive survey endeavors by railroad authorities, a general rule of thumb is that the blocks surveyed by a particular surveyor and at a particular time can be treated as a simultaneous conveyance. In a railroad grant, a block is made of several sections much like the United States Public Land Survey System (PLSS).

Things to remember when apportioning within a simultaneous conveyance/subdivision

- It is used as a "last case resort"; evidence is paramount.
- Never apportion using known erroneous measurements.
- Apportioning should never be extended/carried beyond found monuments.
- Never apportion road width; road widths are set at stated/recorded measurement.
- Only apportion simultaneous conveyances (subdivided lands).
- Process of prorating land equally should be used for land situations where junior and senior rights (sequential conveyances) are not applicable. Never use where junior and senior rights are applicable.
- Where a plan or description leaves a subdivision lot or parcel's dimension unnoted, any deficiency or excess is distributed to that parcel. Unlabeled lot dimensions indicate the allowance of dimension adjustments.
- Where roads/easement exists within a subdivision, their dimensions will never vary if deficiencies or excesses exist. The deficiency and excess is distributed to lots and parcels only. The width of a road should never be apportioned or prorated.
- Bearings yield to distances during the process of apportionment.

Method of single proportioning/prorating

When monument(s) are lost within a simultaneous conveyance the method of proportioning is needed. The concept behind proportioning is comparing measured lengths to recorded lengths. The process is to first establish a ratio between the overall measured length divided by the overall recorded length. The next step is to figure out what portion or percentage of the overall line needs to be reestablished. The final step is to set them equal to each other and solve for the missing element. The ratio of the totals equals the ratio of the proportioned.

First: $\dfrac{measured\ total}{recorded\ total}$ Second: $\dfrac{measured\ portion}{recorded\ portion}$ Third: $\dfrac{measured\ total}{recorded\ total} = \dfrac{measured\ portion}{recorded\ portion}$

Example 1

actual/field verified and measured distance
from A to B = 106′

unknown mid-point

Point A

found monument

recorded distance

from A to B = 100′

Point B

found monument

Total measured distance = 106′
Total recorded distance = 100′

Objective is to reestablish the mid-point between the found monument at point A and the found monument at point B.

Step 1: Set up to ratio of measured vs. recorded distances. In single proportioning this ratio needs to be established in order to prorate that percentage to the proportional length.

$$\dfrac{measured\ total}{recorded\ total}$$

$\dfrac{106′}{100′} = 1.06$ Note: The recorded is smaller than the measured so the ratio is larger than one.

Step 2: establish the percentage/portion of the overall line that needs to be determined. In this instance, the mid-point is needed; meaning half or 50% of the line.

$$\frac{measured\ portion}{recorded\ portion}$$

$\frac{x}{50}$ Note: The measured length is unknown, but the recorded should be 50', because 50' is half of 100'.

Step 3: Set the two proportion ratios (overall and portion) equal to each other and solve for the unknown element.

$$\frac{measured\ total}{recorded\ total} = \frac{measured\ portion}{recorded\ portion}$$

$$\frac{106'}{100'} = \frac{x}{50'}$$
$$1.06 = \frac{x}{50'}$$
$$53' = x$$

The measured distance half-way between the two found monuments is 53'. The distance between the monuments should have been 100' per the record, but when measured the distance was 6' longer. That said, the mid-point should have been 50', but given the 6' "bust" the true mid-point is 53'.

Example 2

Find the location of a monument to be set a quarter of the way between A and B (from point A).

$$\frac{measured\ total}{recorded\ total} = \frac{measured\ portion}{recorded\ portion}$$

$$\frac{106}{100} = \frac{x}{25}$$
$$1.06 = \frac{x}{25}$$
$$26.5 = x$$

Note: The difference between the measured and the recorded divided by the percentage of the length being determined plus the recorded portion will derive the same result.
In the example above: (6'/0.25) + 25 = 26.5'.

EXCESS, DEFICIENCY, VACANCY, AND THE TEXAS SCHOOL FUND

Excess and deficiency

Excess - more land than described.

Deficiency - less land than described.

States favor

Excess and deficiency is in the States favor.

With excess, the grantee owes the State money for the extra land, but is not required to pay for the discovered excess. With deficiency, the landowner only has title to the land described in the conveyance.

March 22, 1889 Act

Patent - title of conveyance by the State.

The March 22, 1889 Act proclaimed that all State patented land was to be re-surveyed in an attempt to recover excesses in previously granted land. These lands were then to be ascertained, distributed, and/or sold, all profits were to be for the School Fund.

The five sections of the act

1) Discovery of the excess were conducted through routine measures (e.g., analysis of survey monumentation).
2) Any excess land were declared property of the State of Texas and placed in the School Fund, the contiguous landowner had a six-month period to purchase the excess.
3) Validation and correction of all surveys occurred.
4) The Act did not apply to any third party acquiring the land in good faith.
5) The Act did not apply to any land previously having patents issued.

Method

Establish lines and corners in even numbered surveys and include the excess acreage allowable to each.

Texas School Fund

The Texas School Fund was originally enacted by the Texas Legislature in 1854. The legislature appropriated $2,000,000 at that time for benefiting Texas public schools. The initial $2,000,000 was provided by the sale of a large area of the Texas territory. In 1876, Texas's new constitution renamed the Texas School Fund to the Permanent School Fund. At that time, half of the public lands in the State were appropriated to the fund. Additionally, the General Land Office was appointed to manage the land and the associated funds. As funds from the sale or lease of public land or mineral royalties (i.e., minerals, oil and gas, and/or other natural resources) are paid, they are added to the School Fund and reinvested for further revenue accumulation. Interest gained is distributed to Texas schools, but the actual principle cannot be spent.

- Officially established 1855-1856
- $10,000,000 were received from the United States as payment for Texas territory of 67 million acres extending into Wyoming, Colorado, New Mexico, and Oklahoma by the Compromise of 1850 ($5,000,000 in bonds and $5,000,000 to settle debts from Texas's annexation into the United States).
- Approximately 44,000,000 acres - mineral rights and leasing rights payments are associated with the permanent school fund
- Approximately 2,000,000 acres - mineral rights and leasing rights payments for the permanent university fund (1,000,000 acres from the original constitutional establishment and an additional 1,000,000 acres from the legislative Act of April 10, 1883).

Vacancies

Vacancy - unsurveyed state land, land yet to be surveyed and segregated from the public domain. Also known as the Public School Fund Land.

The difference between a vacancy and an excess is mainly a factor of whether or not land and adjoining land is surveyed. If the survey line exists and monuments are found/reconstructed vacancies cannot exist, only excesses.

Vacancy hunters - those individuals looking for vacant lands near oil producing sections of land.

Vacancies cannot exist within the interior bounds of a system of surveys or a block. These systems and blocks are to be treated as one overall survey.

A survey system or block is a set of surveys that are:
- Made by the same surveyor.
- Made generally at the same time.
- Surveys calling for one another.
- Made for the same certificate holder.
- Describe a block or system.

MISCELLANEOUS TERMS

Radial survey
- Not recommended - does not meet regulation standards
- Location of multiple features and monuments from one location.
- The occupation of a monument and the foresight/backsight of sequentially ordered monumentation is the correct procedure. The surveyor is required to run round the land located.

Subdivision
Division of land into separate tracts. A tract for each individual owner or joint owners.

Partition
Division of land amongst its joint owners. Partitioning can pertain to multiple, separate tracts.
> Two types of partitioning
>> Voluntary partition - joint owners are in agreement.
>> Judicial partitioning - joint owners are court mandated to partition land.

Cut-out
Splitting off a smaller parcel from a larger, parent tract.

Assumptions of dividing land
It is assumed the division line between the original parcel and the newly created parcel is parallel to the line being "pulled" from.
> Example - <u>North</u> 40 acres of the 100 acre Davis Tract.
>> The division line between the newly created 40 acre tract and the remaining 60 acre tract is assumed to be parallel with the <u>north bound</u> of the original 100 acre Davis Tract, because the "North" 40 acres was called for.

Along vs. with
Along - does not necessarily mean contiguous.
With - implies contact or contiguousness.

Strips and Gores Doctrine

Strip - a narrow piece of land.

Gore - a narrow gap between lands.

The doctrine of "Strips and Gores" is essentially the assumption that a grantor will not purposely or intentionally retain a narrow strip of land during the conveyance of a parcel. The concept is based on the idea that the grantor will not need or have any reasonable purpose for the retention of such a narrow strip of land.

The grantee is given favor regarding strips and gores. Unless however, the strip or gore adjoins the remaining land of the grantor conveying said land.

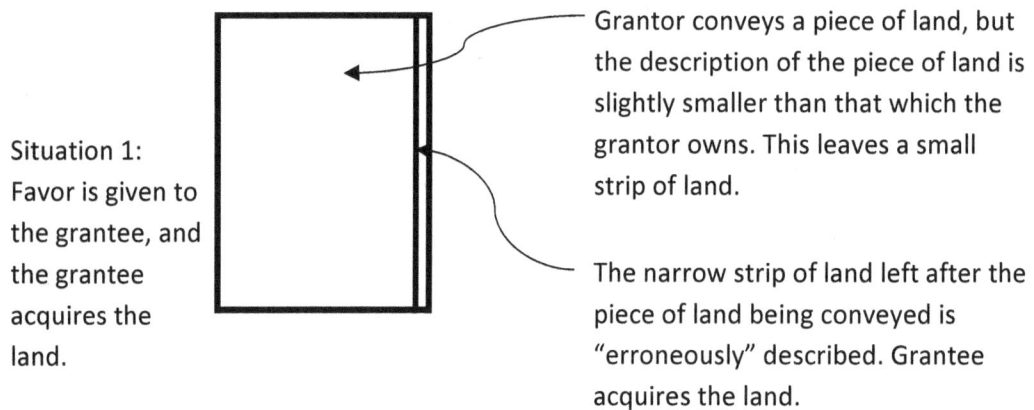

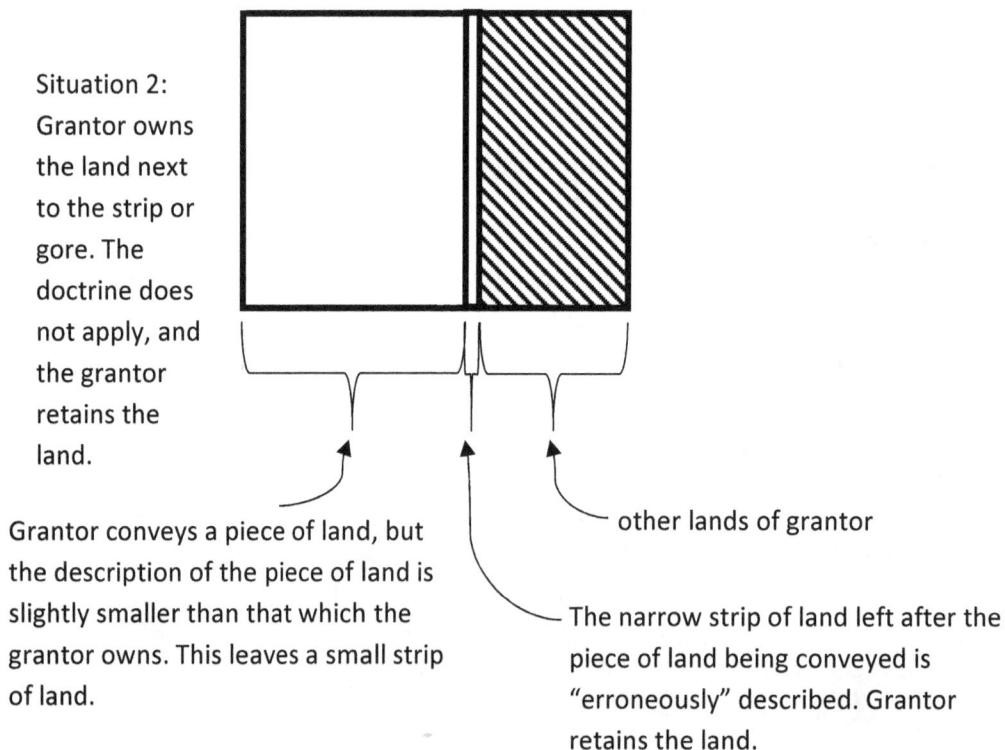

Situation 1: Favor is given to the grantee, and the grantee acquires the land.

Grantor conveys a piece of land, but the description of the piece of land is slightly smaller than that which the grantor owns. This leaves a small strip of land.

The narrow strip of land left after the piece of land being conveyed is "erroneously" described. Grantee acquires the land.

Situation 2: Grantor owns the land next to the strip or gore. The doctrine does not apply, and the grantor retains the land.

Grantor conveys a piece of land, but the description of the piece of land is slightly smaller than that which the grantor owns. This leaves a small strip of land.

other lands of grantor

The narrow strip of land left after the piece of land being conveyed is "erroneously" described. Grantor retains the land.

TEXAS LAND MEASUREMENTS

Vara

A vara is a linear measurement; 33 1/3 inches equal 1 vara ≈ 2.77777 feet equals 1 vara. The vara was introduced as a measurement in the 19th century to measure Spanish land grants. Many surveying contracts for establishing Spanish land grants stipulated the standardized unit of length.

Labor

A labor is an area measurement; 1,000,000 square varas equal 1 labor ≈ 177.1 acres. A labor was used as an area measurement for Spanish land grants throughout Texas and adjoining states. The labor approximates the English system's quarter-section (1/4 of a square mile).

League

A league is an area measurement; 25,000,000 square varas equal 1 league ≈ 4,428.4 acres. A league was used as an area measurement for Spanish land grants throughout Texas and adjoining states. The labor approximates the English system's quarter-section (1/4 of a square mile).

TEXAS SPECIFIC COURT CASES

Texas surveying practices are dictated by findings in several historic court cases. The below noted court cases are among the more significant and well-known cases. The influential court findings associated with these cases govern the practice of land surveying in the State of Texas. The listings below provide the locations and topics associated with each of the court cases:

- **State of Texas v. Heard, 199 S.W. 2d 191, page 33**
  State of Texas v. Heard, 146 Tex. 139, page 40
  State of Texas v. Heard, 204 S.W. 2d 344, page 55
      Topic(s): adverse possession and navigable streams.
- **Humble Oil and Refining Company v. State of Texas, 162 S.W. 2d 119, page 63**
      Topics: vacancies, junior/senior rights, and following the "footsteps" of the original surveyor.
- **State of Texas v. Sulflow, et al., 128 S.W. 652, page 82**
      Topics: rules of dignity/priority of calls and following the "footsteps" of the original surveyor.
- **State of Texas v. E. B. Sullivan, et al., 92 S.W. 288, page 87**
      Topics: ambiguities result from the application of adjoining lands' deeds.
- **Kirby Limber v. T. A. Campbell, 331 S.W. 2d 388, page 96**
      Topics: meander lines and watercourses.
- **Port of Aransas Properties, Inc., et al. v. Ellis, 129 S.W. 2d 699, page 120**
      Topics: riparian rights and accretion.
- **Town of Refugio v. Strauch, 29 S.W. 2d 1041, page 126**
      Topics: use of streets for minerals and non-use of streets does not make them void.
- **Duval County Ranch Company v. Foster, 318 S.W. 2d 25, page 132**
      Topics: parol agreement and acquiescence agreement by mistake invalidates boundary.
- **Stafford v. King, 30 Tex. 257, page 140**
      Topics: rules of dignity/priority of calls, following the "footsteps" of the original surveyor, called for monuments are paramount.
- **Diversion Lake Club v. Heath, 86 S.W. 2d 441, page 160**
      Topics: navigable waterways and public use.
- **Rio Bravo Oil Company, et al. v. J. F. Weed, et al., 50 S.W. 2d 1080, page 169**
      Topics: right-of-way centerlines.
- **Luttes v. State of Texas, 289 S.W. 2d 357, page 179**
  Luttes v. State of Texas, 324 S.W. 2d 167, page 202
      Topics: Shorelines and tidal waters.

CONCLUSION AND REFERENCES

This study manual is aimed to assist in understanding land surveying fundamentals and to progress one's career and path to licensure. The topics within are presented in an organized manner for obtaining a solid understanding and to use as a quick reference.

The material compiled herein is based on experience and land surveying education gained thoughout my career as a Registered Professional Land Surveyor. Additionally, I applied common concepts and ideas from essential land surveying references such as:

- *Black's Law Dictionary.* edited by Bryan A. Garner,11th ed., Thomas Reuters, 2019.

- Brinker, Russell C., and Minnick, Roy. *The Surveying Handbook.* 2nd ed., Chapman & Hall, 1995.

- Gold, Kenneth G. *Selected Texas Statutes and Boundary Decisions for Land Surveyors, Land Title Agents, and Title Attorneys.* 2nd ed., 2009.

- Hermansen, Knud. "SVT221: Boundary Law." Surveying 221, Jan. 2006, University of Maine at Orono. Lecture.

- Robillard, Walter G., et al. *Brown's Boundary Control and Legal Principals.* Wiley, 2003.

- United States, Department of the Interior. 2009. *Manual of Surveying Instructions: For the Survey of the Public Lands of the United States.* Bureau of Land Management. Denver, CO: Government Printing Office.

I strongly recommend acquiring additional material for your own surveying library for studying as well as for everyday use.